JONES & BARTLETT LEARNING   INFORMATION SYSTEMS SECURITY & ASSURANCE SERIES

MW00845313

LABORATORY MANUAL TO AC

Managing Risk in Information Systems

VERSION 2.0

Powered by vLab Solutions

JONES & BARTLETT
LEARNING

World Headquarters
Jones & Bartlett Learning
5 Wall Street
Burlington, MA 01803
978-443-5000
info@jblearning.com
www.jblearning.com

Jones & Bartlett Learning books and products are available through most bookstores and online booksellers. To contact Jones & Bartlett Learning directly, call 800-832-0034, fax 978-443-8000, or visit our website, www.jblearning.com.

Substantial discounts on bulk quantities of Jones & Bartlett Learning publications are available to corporations, professional associations, and other qualified organizations. For details and specific discount information, contact the special sales department at Jones & Bartlett Learning via the above contact information or send an email to specialsales@jblearning.com.

Copyright © 2015 Jones & Bartlett Learning, LLC, an Ascend Learning Company

All rights reserved. No part of the material protected by this copyright may be reproduced or utilized in any form, electronic or mechanical, including photocopying, recording, or by any information storage and retrieval system, without written permission from the copyright owner.

The *Laboratory Manual to accompany Managing Risk in Information Systems, Version 2.0* is an independent publication and has not been authorized, sponsored, or otherwise approved by the owners of the trademarks or service marks referenced in this product. The screenshots in this product are for educational and instructive purposes only. All trademarks displayed are the trademarks of the parties noted therein. Such use of trademarks is not an endorsement by said parties of Jones & Bartlett Learning, its products, or its services, nor should such use be deemed an endorsement by Jones & Bartlett Learning of said third party's products or services.

Microsoft, Internet Explorer, Windows, Microsoft Office, Microsoft Security Development Lifecycle, and Microsoft Baseline Security Analyzer are either registered trademarks or trademarks of Microsoft Corporation in the United States and/or other countries.

This publication is designed to provide accurate and authoritative information in regard to the subject matter covered. It is sold with the understanding that the publisher is not engaged in rendering legal, accounting, or other professional service. If legal advice or other expert assistance is required, the service of a competent professional person should be sought.

Production Credits

Chief Executive Officer: Ty Field
President: James Homer
Chief Product Officer: Eduardo Moura
SVP, Curriculum Solutions: Christopher Will
Director of Sales, Curriculum Solutions: Randi Roger
Author: vLab Solutions, LLC, David Kim, President
Editorial Management: High Stakes Writing, LLC, Lawrence J. Goodrich, President
Copy Editor, High Stakes Writing: Katherine Dillin
Developmental Editor, High Stakes Writing: Dee Hayes

Associate Program Manager: Rainna Erikson
Production Manager: Susan Beckett
Rights & Photo Research Associate: Lauren Miller
Manufacturing and Inventory Control Supervisor: Amy Bacus
Senior Marketing Manager: Andrea DeFronzo
Cover Design: Scott Moden
Cover Image: © HunThomas/ShutterStock, Inc.
Printing and Binding: Edwards Brothers Malloy
Cover Printing: Edwards Brothers Malloy

ISBN: 978-1-284-05868-0

6048

Printed in the United States of America

18 17 16 15 14   10 9 8 7 6 5 4 3 2 1

Contents

Ethics and Your Personal Responsibilities

© Rodolfo Clix/Dreamstime.com

The material presented in this course is designed to give you a real-life look at the use of various tools and systems that are at the heart of every cybersecurity practitioner's daily responsibilities. During this course, you will have access to software and techniques used by professionals to investigate and test the security of critical infrastructures and information technology systems and devices. With this access come certain ethical responsibilities:

1. Do not exceed your authorized level of access. This includes remaining within your authorized level of access when using lab-provided software tools to scan or attack computers and software applications as directed within the lab procedures.

2. Do not attempt to use your authorized access for unauthorized purposes either inside or outside of the VSCL environment.

3. Do not attempt to attack or otherwise compromise the confidentiality, integrity, or availability of *any* IT systems, services, or infrastructures outside of the VSCL.

4. Comply with your academic institution's *Code of Student Conduct* and all other applicable policies and regulations.

5. Comply with applicable federal, state, and local laws regarding the use and misuse of information technology systems and services.

6. Comply with applicable laws regarding intellectual property rights, including patents and trademarks and copyrights.

© Rodolfo Clix/Dreamstime.com

Preface

Welcome! This lab manual is your step-by-step guide to completing the laboratory exercises for this course. You will have an opportunity to gain valuable hands-on experience with professional-grade tools and techniques as you work through the lab activities and answer the lab questions found at the end of each lab.

How to Use This Lab Manual

This lab manual features step-by-step instructions for completing the following hands-on lab exercises:

Lab #	Lab Title
1	Identifying Threats and Vulnerabilities in an IT Infrastructure
2	Aligning Risks, Threats, and Vulnerabilities to COBIT P09 Risk Management Controls
3	Defining the Scope and Structure for an IT Risk Management Plan
4	Performing a Qualitative Risk Assessment for an IT Infrastructure
5	Identifying Risks, Threats, and Vulnerabilities in an IT Infrastructure Using Zenmap® GUI (Nmap) and Nessus® Reports
6	Developing a Risk-Mitigation Plan Outline for an IT Infrastructure
7	Performing a Business Impact Analysis for a Mock IT Infrastructure
8	Developing an Outline for a Business Continuity Plan for an IT Infrastructure
9	Developing Disaster Recovery Backup Procedures and Recovery Instructions
10	Creating a CIRT Response Plan for a Typical IT Infrastructure

Step-by-Step Instructions

For each lab, you are provided with detailed, step-by-step instructions and screen captures showing the results of key steps within the lab. All actions that you are required to take are shown in **bold** font. The screen captures will also help you identify menus, dialog boxes, and input locations.

Deliverables

As you work through each lab, you will be instructed to record specific information or take a screen capture to document the results you obtained by performing specific actions. The deliverables are designed to test your understanding of the information, and your successful completion of the steps and functions of the lab. All of these documentation tasks should be pasted into a single file (MS Word .doc, .docx, or other compatible format) and submitted for grading by your instructor.

You will create two deliverable files for each lab:

- *Lab Report file* (including screen captures taken at specific steps in the lab)
- *Lab Assessment file* (including answers to questions posed at the end of each lab)

You may use either Microsoft® Word or any other compatible word processing software for these deliverables. For specific information on deliverables, refer to the Deliverables section in each lab.

Lab Assessment File

At the end of each lab, there is a set of questions which are to be answered and submitted for grading in the Lab Assessment file. (Your instructor may provide alternate instructions for this deliverable.) For some questions, you may need to refer to your Lab Report file to obtain information from the lab. For other questions, you may need to consult a textbook or other authoritative source to obtain more information.

Web References

URLs for Web resources listed in this laboratory manual are subject to change without prior notice. These links were last verified on May 1, 2014. Many times, you can find the required resource by using an Internet search engine and a partial URL or keywords. You may also search the Internet Archives (also referred to as the "Wayback Machine") for a given URL that is no longer available at the original Web site (http://www.archive.org).

Technical Support

If you need help completing a lab in this manual, contact the Jones & Bartlett Learning Help Desk using the information below. Remember to include the name of your institution and reference the course name and number in your ticket details

Phone: 1-866-601-4525

Online: http://www.jblcourses.com/techsupport

Monday-Thursday:	8AM – 10PM
Friday:	8AM – 8PM
Saturday:	8AM – 5PM
Sunday:	10AM – 11PM
	(All hours are EST)

If you need help outside of these hours, submit an online ticket or leave a message on our toll-free phone line, and someone from the help desk will get back to you as soon as possible.

Credits

Adobe Reader® is a registered trademark of Adobe Systems Incorporated in the United States and/or other countries. Active Directory®, Excel®, Microsoft®, Windows®, and Windows Server® are registered trademarks of Microsoft Corporation in the United States and/or other countries. Linux® is a registered trademark of Linus Torvalds. Citrix® is a registered trademark of Citrix Systems, Inc. and/or one or more of its subsidiaries, and may be registered in the United States Patent and Trademark Office and in other countries. FileZilla® is a registered trademark of Tim Kosse. Firefox® is a registered trademark of the Mozilla Foundation. Nessus® is a registered trademark of Tenable Network Security. NetWitness® is a registered trademark of EMC Corporation in the United States and other countries. Nmap Security Scanner® and Zenmap® are either registered trademarks or trademarks of Insecure.com LLC. Wireshark® is a registered trademark of the Wireshark Foundation. pfSense® is a federally registered trademark of Electric Sheep Fencing LLC. Debian® is a registered trademark of Software in the Public Interest, Inc. Retina® is a registered trademark of BeyondTrust, Inc. Openswan® is an unregistered trademark of Xelerance.

All brand names and product names used in this document are trademarks, registered trademarks, or trade names of their respective holders.

© Rodolfo Clix/Dreamstime.com

Lab #1 Identifying Threats and Vulnerabilities in an IT Infrastructure

Introduction

The task of identifying risks in an IT environment can become overwhelming. Once your mind starts asking "what if…?" about one IT area, you quickly begin to grasp how many vulnerabilities exist across the IT spectrum. It may seem impossible to systematically search for risks across the whole IT environment.

Thankfully, a solution is at hand that simplifies identifying threats and vulnerabilities in an IT infrastructure. That method is to divide the infrastructure into the seven domains: Wide Area Network (WAN), Local Area Network-to-Wide Area Network (LAN-to-WAN), Local Area Network (LAN), Workstation, User, System/Application, and Remote Access. Systematically tackling the seven individual domains of a typical IT infrastructure helps you organize the roles, responsibilities, and accountabilities for risk management and risk mitigation.

In this lab, you will identify known risks, threats, and vulnerabilities, and you will organize them. Finally, you will map these risks to the domain that was impacted from a risk management perspective.

Learning Objectives

Upon completing this lab, you will be able to:

- Identify common risks, threats, and vulnerabilities found throughout the seven domains of a typical IT infrastructure.
- Align risks, threats, and vulnerabilities to one of the seven domains of a typical IT infrastructure.
- Given a scenario, prioritize risks, threats, and vulnerabilities based on their risk impact to the organization from a risk-assessment perspective.
- Prioritize the identified critical, major, and minor risks, threats, and software vulnerabilities found throughout the seven domains of a typical IT infrastructure.

1

Deliverables

Upon completion of this lab, you are required to provide the following deliverables to your instructor:

1. Lab Report file;
2. Lab Assessments file.

Hands-On Steps

> **▶Note:**
> This is a paper-based lab. To successfully complete the deliverables for this lab, you will need access to Microsoft® Word or another compatible word processor. For some labs, you may also need access to a graphics line drawing application, such as Visio or PowerPoint. Refer to the Preface of this manual for information on creating the lab deliverable files.

1. On your local computer, **create** the **lab deliverable files**.

2. **Review** the **Lab Assessment Worksheet**. You will find answers to these questions as you proceed through the lab steps.

3. **Review** the seven domains of a typical IT infrastructure (see Figure 1).

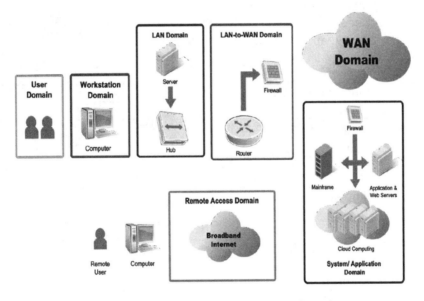

Figure 1 Seven domains of a typical IT infrastructure

4. In your Lab Report file, **describe** how risk can impact each of the seven domains of a typical IT infrastructure: User, Workstation, Local Area Network (LAN), Local Area Network-to-Wide Area Network (LAN-to-WAN), Wide Area Network (WAN), Remote Access, and System/Application domains.

5. **Review** the left-hand column of the following table of risks, threats, and vulnerabilities that were found in a health care IT infrastructure servicing patients with life-threatening conditions:

Copyright © 2015 by Jones & Bartlett Learning, LLC, an Ascend Learning Company. All rights reserved.

Risks, Threats, and Vulnerabilities	Primary Domain Impacted
Unauthorized access from public Internet	
Hacker penetrates IT infrastructure through modem bank	
Communication circuit outages	
Workstation operating system (OS) has a known software vulnerability	
Denial of service attack on organization's e-mail server	
Remote communications from home office	
Workstation browser has software vulnerability	
Weak ingress/egress traffic-filtering degrades performance	
Wireless Local Area Network (WLAN) access points are needed for LAN connectivity within a warehouse	
Need to prevent rogue users from unauthorized WLAN access	
Doctor destroys data in application, deletes all files, and gains access to internal network	
Fire destroys primary data center	
Intraoffice employee romance gone bad	
Loss of production data server	
Unauthorized access to organization-owned workstations	
LAN server OS has a known software vulnerability	
Nurse downloads an unknown e-mail attachment	
Service provider has a major network outage	
A technician inserts CDs and USB hard drives with personal photos, music, and videos on organization-owned computers	
Virtual Private Network (VPN) tunneling between the remote computer and ingress/egress router	

▶**Note:**

Some risks will affect multiple IT domains. In fact, in real-world environments, risks and their direct consequences will most likely span across several domains. This is a big reason to implement controls in more than one domain to mitigate those risks. However, for the exercise in step 6 that follows, consider and select only the domain that would be most affected.

Subsequent next steps in the real world include selecting, implementing, and testing controls to minimize or eliminate those risks. Remember that a risk can be responded to in one of four ways: accept it, treat it (minimize it), avoid it, or transfer it (for example, outsource or insurance).

6. In your Lab Report file, **complete** the table from the previous step by identifying which of the seven domains of a typical IT infrastructure will be most impacted by each item in the table's left-hand column and **explain** why.

> ▶ **Note:**
> This completes the lab. **Close** the **Web browser**, if you have not already done so.

Copyright © 2015 by Jones & Bartlett Learning, LLC, an Ascend Learning Company. All rights reserved.
www.jblearning.com

Evaluation Criteria and Rubrics

The following are the evaluation criteria for this lab that students must perform:

1. Identify common risks, threats, and vulnerabilities found throughout the seven domains of a typical IT infrastructure. – **[25%]**
2. Align risks, threats, and vulnerabilities to one of the seven domains of a typical IT infrastructure. – **[25%]**
3. Given a scenario, prioritize risks, threats, and vulnerabilities based on their risk impact to the organization from a risk-assessment perspective. – **[25%]**
4. Prioritize the identified critical, major, and minor risks, threats, and software vulnerabilities found throughout the seven domains of a typical IT infrastructure. – **[25%]**

Lab #1 - Assessment Worksheet

Identifying Threats and Vulnerabilities in an IT Infrastructure

Course Name and Number: _____

Student Name: _____

Instructor Name: _____

Lab Due Date: _____

Overview

In this lab, you identified known risks, threats, and vulnerabilities, and you organized them. Finally, you mapped these risks to the domain that was impacted from a risk management perspective.

Lab Assessment Questions & Answers

1. Health care organizations must strictly comply with the Health Insurance Portability and Accountability Act (HIPAA) Privacy and Security rules that require organizations to have proper security controls for handling personal information referred to as "protected health information," or PHI. This includes security controls for the IT infrastructure handling PHI. Which of the listed risks, threats, or vulnerabilities can violate HIPAA privacy and security requirements? List one and justify your answer in one or two sentences.

2. How many threats and vulnerabilities did you find that impacted risk in each of the seven domains of a typical IT infrastructure?

3. Which domain(s) had the greatest number of risks, threats, and vulnerabilities?

4. What is the risk impact or risk factor (critical, major, and minor) that you would qualitatively assign to the risks, threats, and vulnerabilities you identified for the LAN-to-WAN Domain for the health care and HIPAA compliance scenario?

Copyright © 2015 by Jones & Bartlett Learning, LLC, an Ascend Learning Company. All rights reserved.
www.jblearning.com

5. Of the three System/Application Domain risks, threats, and vulnerabilities identified, which one requires a disaster recovery plan and business continuity plan to maintain continued operations during a catastrophic outage?

6. Which domain represents the greatest risk and uncertainty to an organization?

7. Which domain requires stringent access controls and encryption for connectivity to corporate resources from home?

8. Which domain requires annual security awareness training and employee background checks for sensitive positions to help mitigate risks from employee sabotage?

9. Which domains need software vulnerability assessments to mitigate risk from software vulnerabilities?

10. Which domain requires acceptable use policies (AUPs) to minimize unnecessary user-initiated Internet traffic and can be monitored and controlled by Web content filters?

11. In which domain do you implement Web content filters?

12. If you implement a Wireless LAN (WLAN) to support connectivity for laptops in the Workstation Domain, which domain does WLAN fall within?

13. Under the Gramm-Leach-Bliley-Act (GLBA), banks must protect customer privacy. A given bank has just implemented its online banking solution that allows customers to access their accounts and perform transactions via their computers or personal digital assistant (PDA) devices. Online banking servers and their public Internet hosting would fall within which domains of security responsibility?

14. True or false: Customers who conduct online banking on their laptops or personal computers must use Hypertext Transfer Protocol Secure (HTTPS), the secure and encrypted version of Hypertext Transfer Protocol (HTTP) browser communications. HTTPS encrypts Web page data inputs and data through the public Internet and decrypts that Web page and data on the user's PC or device.

15. Explain how a layered security strategy throughout the seven domains of a typical IT infrastructure can help mitigate risk exposure for loss of privacy data or confidential data from the System/Application Domain.

Copyright © 2015 by Jones & Bartlett Learning, LLC, an Ascend Learning Company. All rights reserved.
www.jblearning.com

© Rodolfo Clix/Dreamstime.com

Lab #2 Aligning Risks, Threats, and Vulnerabilities to COBIT P09 Risk Management Controls

Introduction

Ask any IT manager about the challenges in conveying IT risks in terms of business risks, or about translating business goals into IT goals. It's a common difficulty, as the worlds of business and IT do not inherently align. This lack of alignment was unresolved until ISACA developed a framework called COBIT, first released in 1996. ISACA is an IT professionals' association centered on auditing and IT governance. This lab will focus on the COBIT framework. The lab uses the latest two versions: COBIT 4.1, which is currently the most implemented version, and COBIT 5, which is the latest version released in June 2012.

Because COBIT 4.1 is freely available at the time of this writing, the lab uses this version to present handling of risk management. Presentation is done making use of a set of COBIT control objectives called P09. COBIT P09's purpose is to guide the scope of risk management for an IT infrastructure. The COBIT P09 risk management controls help organize the identified risks, threats, and vulnerabilities, enabling you to manage and remediate them. This lab will also present how COBIT shifts from the term "control objectives" to a set of principles and enablers in version 5.

In this lab, you will define COBIT P09, you will describe COBIT P09's six control objectives, you will explain how the threats and vulnerabilities align to the definition for the assessment and management of risks, and you will use COBIT P09 to determine the scope of risk management for an IT infrastructure.

Learning Objectives

Upon completing this lab, you will be able to:

- Define what COBIT (Control Objectives for Information and related Technology) P09 risk management is for an IT infrastructure.
- Describe COBIT P09's six control objectives that are used as benchmarks for IT risk assessment and risk management.
- Explain how threats and vulnerabilities align to the COBIT P09 risk management definition for the assessment and management of IT risks.
- Use the COBIT P09 controls as a guide to define the scope of risk management for an IT infrastructure.
- Apply the COBIT P09 controls to help organize the identified IT risks, threats, and vulnerabilities.

Deliverables

Upon completion of this lab, you are required to provide the following deliverables to your instructor:

1. Lab Report file;
2. Lab Assessments file.

Copyright © 2015 by Jones & Bartlett Learning, LLC, an Ascend Learning Company. All rights reserved.
www.jblearning.com

Hands-On Steps

> ▶**Note:**
> This is a paper-based lab. To successfully complete the deliverables for this lab, you will need access to Microsoft® Word or another compatible word processor. For some labs, you may also need access to a graphics line drawing application, such as Visio or PowerPoint. Refer to the Preface of this manual for information on creating the lab deliverable files.

1. On your local computer, **create** the **lab deliverable files**.

2. **Review** the **Lab Assessment Worksheet**. You will find answers to these questions as you proceed through the lab steps.

3. **Review** the seven domains of a typical IT infrastructure (see Figure 1).

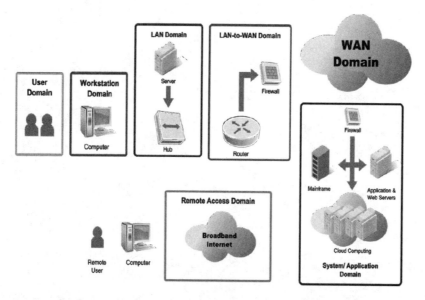

Figure 1 Seven domains of a typical IT infrastructure

4. On your local computer, **open** a new **Internet browser window**.

5. In the address box of your Internet browser, **type** the URL **http://www.isaca.org/Knowledge-Center/cobit/Pages/FAQ.aspx and press Enter to open the Web site**.

6. **Review** the information on the COBIT FAQs page.

ISACA—45 Years Serving Auditors and Business

ISACA is a global organization that defines the roles of information systems governance, security, auditing, and assurance professionals worldwide. ISACA standardizes a level of understanding of these areas through two well-known certifications, the Certified Information Systems Auditor (CISA) and Certified Information Security Manager (CISM). In recent years, ISACA has expanded its certification offerings to include two other certifications around risk and IT governance.

ISACA was previously an acronym expanding to Information Systems Audit and Control Association, but today is known by the name ISACA alone to better serve its wider audience.

Similarly, COBIT was originally an acronym for Control Objectives for Information and related Technology. Now, ISACA refers to the framework as just COBIT, in part because the concept of "control objectives" ends with COBIT version 4.1. COBIT 5 focuses on business-centric concepts and definitions, distinguishes between governance and management, and includes a product family of "enabler guides" and "practice guides." The recent release of COBIT version 5 is a complete break from COBIT 4. In addition, COBIT 5 also incorporates other ISACA products, including Val IT and Risk IT.

7. In your Lab Report file, **describe** the primary goal of the COBIT v4.1 Framework. **Define COBIT**.

8. On the left side of the COBIT Web site, **click** the **COBIT 4.1 Controls Collaboration link**.

9. At the top of the page, **read** about the COBIT Controls area within ISACA's Knowledge Center.

10. In your Lab Report file, **describe** the major objective of the Controls area.

11. **Scroll down** the Web page to the COBIT Domains and Control Objectives section.

12. **Click** the **Text View tab**.

13. In your Lab Report file, **list** each of the types of **control objectives** and briefly **describe** them based on the descriptions on the Web site. Include the following:

   - Plan and Organize
   - Acquire and Implement
   - Monitor and Evaluate
   - Delivery and Support
   - Process Controls
   - Application Controls

14. On the Web site, under the Plan and Organize Control Objective description, **click** the **View all the PO Control Objectives link**.

Copyright © 2015 by Jones & Bartlett Learning, LLC, an Ascend Learning Company. All rights reserved.
www.jblearning.com

15. **Scroll down** and find the **P09 Control Objectives**, which are labeled Assess and Manage IT Risks.

> ▶**Note:**
> COBIT 5 is not an evolutionary but a revolutionary change. Naturally, risk management is covered, but it is done in a holistic, end-to-end business approach, rather than in an IT-centered approach.

16. **Click** the **P09.1, IT Risk Management Framework link**.

17. **Scroll down** to about the middle of the page to **read** about the IT Risk Management Framework.

18. **Expand** the **View value and Risk Drivers** and **View Control Practices links** to learn more.

19. In your Lab Report file, **describe** what this objective covers.

20. **Click** the other **P09 Control Objectives** by first **clicking** the **back button** to return to the COBIT Domains and Control Objectives section of the COBIT 4.1 Controls Collaboration page.

21. **Click** the **Text View tab**.

22. **Click** the **View all the PO Control Objectives link**.

23. **Scroll down** to the **P09 Control Objectives**.

24. Finally, **click** the **P09.2, Establishment of Risk Context link**.

25. **Repeat** this set of instructions for each of the other P09 listings.

26. **Read** about each of these.

27. In your Lab Report file, **explain** how you use the P09 Control Objectives to organize identified IT risks, threats, and vulnerabilities so you can then manage and remediate the risks, threats, and vulnerabilities in a typical IT infrastructure.

> ▶**Note:**
> This completes the lab. **Close** the **Web browser**, if you have not already done so.

Evaluation Criteria and Rubrics

The following are the evaluation criteria for this lab that students must perform:

1. Define what COBIT (Control Objectives for Information and related Technology) P09 risk management is for an IT infrastructure. – **[20%]**
2. Describe COBIT P09's six control objectives that are used as benchmarks for IT risk assessment and risk management. – **[20%]**
3. Explain how threats and vulnerabilities align to the COBIT P09 risk management definition for the assessment and management of IT risks. – **[20%]**
4. Use the COBIT P09 controls as a guide to define the scope of risk management for an IT infrastructure. – **[20%]**
5. Apply the COBIT P09 controls to help organize the identified IT risks, threats, and vulnerabilities. – **[20%]**

Copyright © 2015 by Jones & Bartlett Learning, LLC, an Ascend Learning Company. All rights reserved.

Lab #2 - Assessment Worksheet

Aligning Risks, Threats, and Vulnerabilities to COBIT P09 Risk Management Controls

Course Name and Number: _____

Student Name: _____

Instructor Name: _____

Lab Due Date: _____

Overview

In this lab, you defined COBIT P09, you described COBIT P09's six control objectives, you explained how the threats and vulnerabilities align to the definition for the assessment and management of risks, and you used COBIT P09 to determine the scope of risk management for an IT infrastructure.

Lab Assessment Questions & Answers

1. What is COBIT P09's purpose?

2. Name three of COBIT's six control objectives.

3. For each of the threats and vulnerabilities from the Identifying Threats and Vulnerabilities in an IT Infrastructure lab in this lab manual (list at least three and no more than five) that you have remediated, what must you assess as part of your overall COBIT P09 risk management approach for your IT infrastructure?

4. True or false: COBIT P09 risk management control objectives focus on assessment and management of IT risk.

5. What is the name of the organization that defined the COBIT P09 Risk Management Framework?

6. Describe three of the COBIT P09 control objectives.

7. Describe three of the COBIT P09.1 IT Risk Management Framework control objectives.

Copyright © 2015 by Jones & Bartlett Learning, LLC, an Ascend Learning Company. All rights reserved.
www.jblearning.com

Lab #3 Defining the Scope and Structure for an IT Risk Management Plan

Introduction

Every company needs to take risks to thrive, but not too much risk which could be catastrophic. Finding the balanced amount of risk requires identifying what opportunities (or threats) are present, understanding how significant each of them is, recognizing what action to take to smartly handle both opportunities and risks, and lastly, monitoring all of the above, including discovering more prospects and threats. All told, this is called risk management. Specific to the seven domains of the IT infrastructure, this lab will cover IT risk management.

In this lab, you will define the purpose of an IT risk management plan, you will define the scope for an IT risk management plan that encompasses the seven domains of a typical IT infrastructure, you will relate the risks, threats, and vulnerabilities to the plan, and you will create an IT risk management plan outline that incorporates the five major parts of an IT risk management process.

Learning Objectives

Upon completing this lab, you will be able to:

- Define the purpose and objectives of an IT risk management plan.
- Define the scope and boundary for an IT risk management plan to encompass the seven domains of a typical IT infrastructure.
- Relate identified risks, threats, and vulnerabilities to an IT risk management plan and risk areas.
- Incorporate the five major parts of an IT risk management process into a risk management plan's outline.
- Craft an outline for an IT risk management plan, which includes the seven domains of a typical IT infrastructure and the five major parts of risk management and risk areas.

Deliverables

Upon completion of this lab, you are required to provide the following deliverables to your instructor:

1. Lab Report file;
2. Lab Assessments file.

Copyright © 2015 by Jones & Bartlett Learning, LLC, an Ascend Learning Company. All rights reserved.

Hands-On Steps

> **▶ Note:**
> This is a paper-based lab. To successfully complete the deliverables for this lab, you will need access to Microsoft® Word or another compatible word processor. For some labs, you may also need access to a graphics line drawing application, such as Visio or PowerPoint. Refer to the Preface of this manual for information on creating the lab deliverable files.

1. On your local computer, **create** the **lab deliverable files**.

2. **Review** the **Lab Assessment Worksheet**. You will find answers to these questions as you proceed through the lab steps.

3. On your local computer, **open** a new **Internet browser window**.

4. Using your favorite search engine, **search for information** on the **IT risk management process**.

5. **Briefly review** at least five of the first page results.

6. In the address box of your Internet browser, **type** the URL **http://www.uvm.edu/~erm/RiskAssessmentGuide.pdf and press Enter to open the Web site.**

7. **Review** the PDF titled "Guide to Risk Assessment & Response."

> **▶ Note:**
> Take special note of the University of Vermont's "Guide to Risk Assessment & Response" document and the insightful sections titled "Things to Keep in Mind" and "Steps to Follow" for each of the assessment steps.

8. In the address box of your Internet browser, **type** the URL **http://www.education.nt.gov.au/__data/assets/pdf_file/0011/4106/risk_management_process .pdf and press Enter to open the Web site.**

9. **Review** the PowerPoint slide deck titled "The Risk Management Process."

10. In your Lab Report file, **describe** in what ways the risk management process in both IT and non-IT environments are similar. Briefly describe in your own words the five major steps of risk management: plan, identify, assess, respond, and monitor.

11. In your Lab Report file, **describe** the plan.

12. **Review** the seven domains of a typical IT infrastructure (see Figure 1).

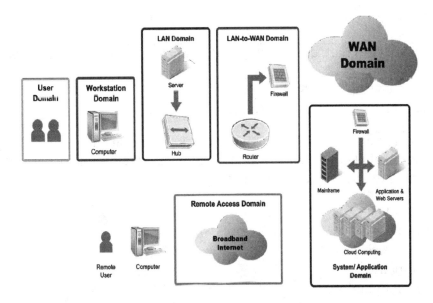

Figure 1 Seven domains of a typical IT infrastructure

13. Using the following table of risks, threats, and vulnerabilities that were found in a health care IT infrastructure servicing patients with life-threatening conditions, **review** the risks in the following table. **Consider** how you might manage each risk and which of the seven domains each one affects:

Risks, Threats, and Vulnerabilities
Unauthorized access from public Internet
Hacker penetrates IT infrastructure
Communication circuit outages
Workstations
Workstation operating system (OS) has a known software vulnerability
Denial of service attack on organization's e-mail
Remote communications from home office
Workstation browser has software vulnerability
Weak ingress/egress traffic-filtering degrades performance
Wireless Local Area Network (WLAN) access points are needed for Local Area Network (LAN) connectivity within a warehouse
Need to prevent rogue users from unauthorized WLAN access
User destroys data in application, deletes all files, and gains access to internal network
Fire destroys primary data center
Intraoffice employee romance gone bad
Loss of production data server
Unauthorized access to organization-owned workstations
LAN server OS has a known software vulnerability
User downloads an unknown e-mail attachment
Service provider has a major network outage

Copyright © 2015 by Jones & Bartlett Learning, LLC, an Ascend Learning Company. All rights reserved.
www.jblearning.com

User inserts CDs and USB hard drives with personal photos, music, and videos on organization-owned computers
Virtual Private Network (VPN) tunneling between the remote computer and ingress/egress router

14. In your Lab Report file, for each of the domains, **create** an outline in the scope of your risk management plan. Include the following topics—the five major parts of an IT risk management process—for each domain:

- Risk planning
- Risk identification
- Risk assessment
- Risk response
- Risk monitoring

▶ **Note:**
This completes the lab. **Close** the **Web browser**, if you have not already done so.

Evaluation Criteria and Rubrics

The following are the evaluation criteria for this lab that students must perform:

1. Define the purpose and objectives of an IT risk management plan. – **[20%]**
2. Define the scope and boundary for an IT risk management plan to encompass the seven domains of a typical IT infrastructure. – **[20%]**
3. Relate identified risks, threats, and vulnerabilities to an IT risk management plan and risk areas. – **[20%]**
4. Incorporate the five major parts of an IT risk management process into a risk management plan's outline. – **[20%]**
5. Craft an outline for an IT risk management plan, which includes the seven domains of a typical IT infrastructure and the five major parts of risk management and risk areas. – **[20%]**

Copyright © 2015 by Jones & Bartlett Learning, LLC, an Ascend Learning Company. All rights reserved.

Lab #3 - Assessment Worksheet

Defining the Scope and Structure for an IT Risk Management Plan

Course Name and Number: _____

Student Name: _____

Instructor Name: _____

Lab Due Date: _____

Overview

In this lab, you defined the purpose of an IT risk management plan, you defined the scope for an IT risk management plan that encompasses the seven domains of a typical IT infrastructure, you related the risks, threats, and vulnerabilities to the plan, and you created an IT risk management plan outline that incorporates the five major parts of an IT risk management process.

Lab Assessment Questions & Answers

1. What is the goal or objective of an IT risk management plan?

2. What are the five fundamental components of an IT risk management plan?

3. Define what risk planning is.

4. What is the first step in performing risk management?

5. What is the exercise called when you are trying to gauge how significant a risk is?

6. What practice helps address a risk?

7. What ongoing practice helps track risk in real time?

8. True or False: Once a company completes all risk management steps (identification, assessment, response, and monitoring), the task is done.

9. Given that an IT risk management plan can be large in scope, why is it a good idea to develop a risk management plan team?

10. In the seven domains of a typical IT infrastructure, which domain is the most difficult to plan, identify, assess, treat, and monitor?

11. Which compliance laws or standards does the health care organization mentioned in the Hands-On Steps have to comply with (consider these: Health Insurance Portability and Accountability Act [HIPAA], Gramm-Leach-Bliley Act [GLBA], and Family Educational Rights and Privacy Act [FERPA])? How does this impact the scope and boundary of its IT risk management plan?

12. How did the risk identification and risk assessment of the identified risks, threats, and vulnerabilities contribute to your IT risk management plan outline?

13. What risks, threats, and vulnerabilities did you identify and assess that require immediate risk mitigation given the criticality of the threat or vulnerability?

14. For risk monitoring, what are some techniques or tools you can implement in each of the seven domains of a typical IT infrastructure to help mitigate risk?

Copyright © 2015 by Jones & Bartlett Learning, LLC, an Ascend Learning Company. All rights reserved.
www.jblearning.com

15. For risk mitigation, what processes and procedures can help streamline and implement risk-mitigation solutions to the production IT infrastructure?

16. What is the purpose of a risk register?

17. How does risk response impact change control management and vulnerability management?

© Rodolfo Clix/Dreamstime.com

Lab #4 Performing a Qualitative Risk Assessment for an IT Infrastructure

Introduction

Risk management begins with first identifying risks, threats, and vulnerabilities to then assess them. Assessing risks means to evaluate risk in terms of two factors. First, evaluate each risk's likelihood of occurring. Second, evaluate the impact or consequences should the risk occur. Both likelihood and impact are important for understanding how each risk measures up to other risks. How the risks compare with one other is important when deciding which risk or risks take priority. In short, assessing is a critical step toward the goal of mitigation.

Assessing risks can be done in one of two ways: quantitatively or qualitatively. Quantitatively means to assign numerical values or some objective, empirical value. For example, "Less than $1,000 to repair" or "Biweekly." Qualitatively means to assign wording or some quasi-subjective value. For example, a risk could be labeled critical, major, or minor.

In this lab, you will define the purpose of an IT risk assessment, you will align identified risks, threats, and vulnerabilities to an IT risk assessment that encompasses the seven domains of a typical IT infrastructure, you will classify the risks, threats, and vulnerabilities, and you will prioritize them. Finally, you will write an executive summary that addresses the risk assessment findings, risk assessment impact, and recommendations to remediate areas of noncompliance.

Learning Objectives

Upon completing this lab, you will be able to:

- Define the purpose and objectives of an IT risk assessment.
- Align identified risks, threats, and vulnerabilities to an IT risk assessment that encompasses the seven domains of a typical IT infrastructure.
- Classify identified risks, threats, and vulnerabilities according to a qualitative risk assessment template.
- Prioritize classified risks, threats, and vulnerabilities according to the defined qualitative risk assessment scale.
- Craft an executive summary that addresses the risk assessment findings, risk assessment impact, and recommendations to remediate areas of noncompliance.

Deliverables

Upon completion of this lab, you are required to provide the following deliverables to your instructor:

1. Lab Report file;
2. Lab Assessments file.

Hands-On Steps

> ▶ **Note:**
> This is a paper-based lab. To successfully complete the deliverables for this lab, you will need access to Microsoft®
> Word or another compatible word processor. For some labs, you may also need access to a graphics line drawing
> application, such as Visio or PowerPoint. Refer to the Preface of this manual for information on creating the lab
> deliverable files.

1. On your local computer, **create** the **lab deliverable files**.

2. **Review** the **Lab Assessment Worksheet**. You will find answers to these questions as you proceed through the lab steps.

3. On your local computer, **open** a new **Internet browser window**.

4. Using your favorite search engine, **search for information** on the **purpose of IT risk assessment**.

5. In your Lab Report file, **describe** the purpose of IT risk assessment.

6. **Review** the following table for the risks, threats, and vulnerabilities found in a health care IT infrastructure servicing patients with life-threatening conditions:

Risks, Threats, and Vulnerabilities	Primary Domain Impacted	Risk Impact/ Factor
Unauthorized access from public Internet		
User destroys data in application and deletes all files		
Hacker penetrates your IT infrastructure and gains access to your internal network		
Intraoffice employee romance gone bad		
Fire destroys primary data center		
Service provider service level agreement (SLA) is not achieved		
Workstation operating system (OS) has a known software vulnerability		
Unauthorized access to organization-owned workstations		
Loss of production data		
Denial of service attack on organization Demilitarized Zone (DMZ) and e-mail server		
Remote communications from home office		
Local Area Network (LAN) server OS has a		

Copyright © 2015 by Jones & Bartlett Learning, LLC, an Ascend Learning Company. All rights reserved.

known software vulnerability		
User downloads and clicks on an unknown e-mail attachment		
Workstation browser has a software vulnerability		
Mobile employee needs secure browser access to sales-order entry system		
Service provider has a major network outage		
Weak ingress/egress traffic-filtering degrades performance		
User inserts CDs and USB hard drives with personal photos, music, and videos on organization-owned computers		
Virtual Private Network (VPN) tunneling between remote computer and ingress/egress router is needed		
Wireless Local Area Network (WLAN) access points are needed for LAN connectivity within a warehouse		
Need to prevent eavesdropping on WLAN due to customer privacy data access		
Denial of service (DoS)/distributed denial of service (DDoS) attack from the Wide Area Network (WAN)/Internet		

7. **Review** the seven domains of a typical IT infrastructure (see Figure 1).

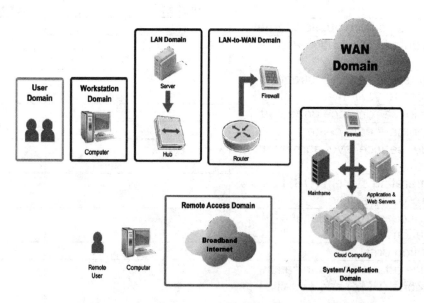

Figure 1 Seven domains of a typical IT infrastructure

8. In your Lab Report file, using the table from step 6, **identify** in the table's Primary Domain Impacted column which of the seven domains of a typical IT infrastructure will be most impacted by each risk, threat, or vulnerability listed.

Qualitative Versus Quantitative

The next step requests that you assign a score to each of the risks in the table from step 6. The scoring is done qualitatively, by assigning one of several labels on a scale. In this case, the scale is provided for you, ranging from Critical to Minor.

Using qualitative scores to assess risks is comparatively easy and quick. The alternative is to assess quantitatively, using actual, numerical scores. Using qualitative words such as "critical" or "major" introduces subjective opinion, while citing numbers such as "Damage to be more than $3 million" or "Will cause an outage of under four hours" introduces quantitative objectivity.

Quantitative scoring is more objective, but calculating risk assessment this way can take much more time. This is because it requires you to dig up hard facts. For instance, you can conduct quantitative scoring by referring to your organization's history or claims records by answering such questions as "How often has this happened to us, or others?" You can also assess risks numerically by researching the costs to recover from losses.

It is possible to assess risks both quantitatively and qualitatively. For example, you could quantitatively score the likelihood and consequences of each risk, for example, "under 10% chance" and " 'X' number of staff lives harmed or lost." But you could present the final score qualitatively, for example, "critical" or "needs to be addressed immediately."

9. In your Lab Report file, using the table from step 6, **perform** a qualitative risk assessment by assigning a risk impact/risk factor to each of the identified risks, threats, and vulnerabilities throughout the seven domains of a typical IT infrastructure where the risk, threat, or vulnerability resides. **Assign** each risk, threat, and vulnerability a priority number in the table's Risk Impact/Factor column, where:

- **"1" is Critical:** A risk, threat, or vulnerability that impacts compliance (that is, privacy law requirement for securing privacy data and implementing proper security controls, and so on) and places the organization in a position of increased liability
- **"2" is Major:** A risk, threat, or vulnerability that impacts the confidentiality, integrity, and availability (C-I-A) of an organization's intellectual property assets and IT infrastructure
"3" is Minor: A risk, threat, or vulnerability that can impact user or employee productivity or availability of the IT infrastructure

▶ Note:

Keep the following in mind when working on the next step: When suggesting next steps to executive management, consider your recommendations from their point of view. Be prepared to explain costs, both in implementing the controls and then in maintaining the controls.

Remember that costs come in many forms, not least of which is labor. Be sure accountability is thought out in terms of roles and responsibilities. Other potential costs outside the data center include goodwill or reputation, market share, and lost opportunity. Executive management might have these costs topmost in mind.

Copyright © 2015 by Jones & Bartlett Learning, LLC, an Ascend Learning Company. All rights reserved.
www.jblearning.com

10. In your Lab Report file, **write** a four-paragraph **executive summary** according to the following outline:

- **Paragraph #1:** Summary of findings (risks, threats, and vulnerabilities found throughout the seven domains of a typical IT infrastructure)
- **Paragraph #2:** Approach and prioritization of critical, major, and minor risk assessment elements
- **Paragraph #3:** Risk assessment and risk impact summary of the seven domains of a typical IT infrastructure
- **Paragraph #4:** Recommendations and next steps for executive management

▶ **Note:**
This completes the lab. **Close** the **Web browser**, if you have not already done so.

Evaluation Criteria and Rubrics

The following are the evaluation criteria for this lab that students must perform:

1. Define the purpose and objectives of an IT risk assessment. – **[20%]**
2. Align identified risks, threats, and vulnerabilities to an IT risk assessment that encompasses the seven domains of a typical IT infrastructure. – **[20%]**
3. Classify identified risks, threats, and vulnerabilities according to a qualitative risk assessment template. – **[20%]**
4. Prioritize classified risks, threats, and vulnerabilities according to the defined qualitative risk assessment scale. – **[20%]**
5. Craft an executive summary that addresses the risk assessment findings, risk assessment impact, and recommendations to remediate areas of noncompliance. – **[20%]**

Copyright © 2015 by Jones & Bartlett Learning, LLC, an Ascend Learning Company. All rights reserved.
www.jblearning.com

Lab #4 - Assessment Worksheet

Performing a Qualitative Risk Assessment for an IT Infrastructure

Course Name and Number: _____

Student Name: _____

Instructor Name: _____

Lab Due Date: _____

Overview

In this lab, you defined the purpose of an IT risk assessment, you aligned identified risks, threats, and vulnerabilities to an IT risk assessment that encompasses the seven domains of a typical IT infrastructure, you classified the risks, threats, and vulnerabilities, and you prioritized them. Finally, you wrote an executive summary that addresses the risk assessment findings, risk assessment impact, and recommendations to remediate areas of noncompliance.

Lab Assessment Questions & Answers

1. What is an IT risk assessment's goal or objective?

2. Why is it difficult to conduct a quantitative risk assessment for an IT infrastructure?

3. What was your rationale in assigning a "1" risk impact/risk factor value of "Critical" to an identified risk, threat, or vulnerability?

4. After you had assigned the "1," "2," and "3" risk impact/risk factor values to the identified risks, threats, and vulnerabilities, how did you prioritize the "1," "2," and "3" risk elements? What would you say to executive management about your final recommended prioritization?

5. Identify a risk-mitigation solution for each of the following risk factors:

    a. User downloads and clicks on an unknown e-mail attachment
    b. Workstation OS has a known software vulnerability
    c. Need to prevent eavesdropping on WLAN due to customer privacy data access
    d. Weak ingress/egress traffic-filtering degrades performance
    e. DoS/DDoS attack from the WAN/Internet
    f. Remote access from home office
    g. Production server corrupts database

Copyright © 2015 by Jones & Bartlett Learning, LLC, an Ascend Learning Company. All rights reserved.
www.jblearning.com

© Rodolfo Clix/Dreamstime.com

Lab #5 Identifying Risks, Threats, and Vulnerabilities in an IT Infrastructure Using Zenmap® GUI (Nmap) and Nessus® Reports

Introduction

Imagine a system administrator learns of a server's vulnerability, and a service patch is available to solve it. Unfortunately, simply applying a patch to a server is not assurance enough that a risk has been mitigated. The system admin has the option of opening the application and verifying that the patch has raised the version number as expected. Still, the admin has no guarantee the vulnerability is closed, at least not until the vulnerability is directly tested. That's what vulnerability scanners are for.

Two vulnerability scanners available to the system administrator are Nmap® and Nessus®, which produce scan reports. The purpose of using Zenmap® GUI (Nmap) and Nessus® reports is to enable you to create network discovery port scanning reports and vulnerability reports. These reports can identify the hosts, operating systems, services, applications, and open ports that are at risk in an organization.

In this lab, you will look at an Nmap® report and a Nessus® report. You will visit the *http://cve.mitre.org* Web site, you will define vulnerability and exposure according to the site, and you will learn how to conduct searches of the Common Vulnerabilities and Exposures (CVE) listing.

Learning Objectives

Upon completing this lab, you will be able to:

- Review a Zenmap® GUI (Nmap) network discovery and port scanning report and a Nessus® software vulnerability report.
- Identify hosts, operating systems, services, applications, and open ports on devices from the Zenmap® GUI (Nmap) scan report.
- Identify critical, major, and minor software vulnerabilities from the Nessus® vulnerability assessment scan report.
- Visit the Common Vulnerabilities and Exposures (CVE) online listing of software vulnerabilities at *http://cve.mitre.org* and learn how to conduct searches on the site.

Deliverables

Upon completion of this lab, you are required to provide the following deliverables to your instructor:

1. Lab Report file;
2. Lab Assessments file.

Copyright © 2015 by Jones & Bartlett Learning, LLC, an Ascend Learning Company. All rights reserved.
www.jblearning.com

Hands-On Steps

> **▶ Note:**
> This is a paper-based lab. To successfully complete the deliverables for this lab, you will need access to Microsoft® Word or another compatible word processor. For some labs, you may also need access to a graphics line drawing application, such as Visio or PowerPoint. Refer to the Preface of this manual for information on creating the lab deliverable files.

1. On your local computer, **create** the **lab deliverable files**.

2. **Review** the **Lab Assessment Worksheet**. You will find answers to these questions as you proceed through the lab steps.

3. **Review** the **Lab 5 Nmap Scan Report** that accompanies this lab.

4. In your Lab Report file, using the Lab 5 Nmap Scan Report, **answer** the following questions:

   - What are the date and timestamp of the Nmap host scan?
   - What is the total number of loaded scripts for scanning?
   - A synchronize packet (SYN) stealth scan discovers all open ports on the targeted host. How many ports are open on the targeted host for the SYN stealth scan at 13:36?
   - Identify hosts, operating systems, services, applications, and open ports on devices from the Zenmap GUI (Nmap) scan report.

Why Nmap Became Popular

Nmap started more than 15 years ago as a simple, command-line tool. Its one purpose—to send crafted packets to a targeted Internet Protocol (IP) address to determine what ports are listening for connections. Knowing what specific ports are listening, the Nmap operator can infer what services are running.

For example, if Transmission Control Protocol (TCP) port 80 is open and listening, it's a safe assumption the target machine is a Web server, running the Hypertext Transfer Protocol (HTTP) service on port 80. Other popular ports such as 21, 25, 137, and 161 mean the services File Transfer Protocol (FTP), Simple Mail Transfer Protocol (SMTP), Network Basic Input/Output System (NetBIOS), and Simple Network Management Protocol (SNMP) are listening, respectively. This made Nmap very popular with administrators who could then monitor and verify their systems' services.

Nmap also became very popular as an easy tool for reconnaissance. With malicious intent, a person armed with knowing what services were running could research what vulnerabilities to exploit. The fast scanning Nmap made locating the recently discovered exploits called zero-day exploits very efficient.

Over the past 15 years, the features available in Nmap have multiplied several times. The ability to craft packets down to specific flags and options can make troubleshooting—and disrupting—networked devices almost limitless. The people and companies tasked with protecting against hackers must play a game of cat and mouse against the growing set of options in tools such as Nmap. Innovation and open source allows this game to be played indefinitely.

5. **Review** the **Lab 5 Nessus Vulnerability Scan Report** that accompanies this lab.

6. In your Lab Report file, using the **Lab 5 Nessus Vulnerability Scan Report, answer** the following questions:

- How many hosts were scanned?
- What were the start and end times for each of the scans?
- How many total vulnerabilities were discovered for each host?
- How many of the vulnerabilities were critical, major, and minor software vulnerabilities?

▶**Note:**

Nessus is a powerful vulnerability scanner, with a fast-growing list of available plug-ins. As a vulnerability scanner, the tool scans the networked devices for potential weaknesses and exploitable services. As you see from the lab sample, reporting can be detailed and customized. While still free for personal, home use, Nessus is also available for commercial use with an annual subscription fee.

Nessus can be installed and run fairly easily, but here are a few tips that will produce much more benefit. First, update the plug-ins on install. By default, Nessus will update plug-ins once a day. Another tip is to use Nessus as a compliance tool. While it is by nature a vulnerability tool, one Nessus feature is to load a configuration file (called an audit file by Nessus) and then scan with Nessus to verify compliance against your end devices.

7. On your local computer, **open** a new **Internet browser window**.

8. In the address box of your Internet browser, **type** the URL **http://cve.mitre.org** and **press Enter** to open the Web site.

9. On the Web site, toward the top left of the screen, **click** the **CVE List link**.

10. **Review** the **CVE List Main Page**.

11. In your Lab Report file, **define CVE**.

12. On the left, under **About CVE, click** the **Terminology link**.

13. **Review** the definitions for **vulnerability** and **exposure**.

14. In your Lab Report file, **define** the terms **vulnerability** and **exposure**.

15. At the top right of the Web site, **click** the **Search link**.

Copyright © 2015 by Jones & Bartlett Learning, LLC, an Ascend Learning Company. All rights reserved.

16. In the Search box, **type** the words **Microsoft® XP 2003 Service Pack 1** and **click the Search button**.

17. In your Lab Report file, **describe** some of the results you discover.

18. After viewing the results, **conduct** another search and this time, **type** the words **Cisco ASA 5505 Security +** and **click the Search button**.

19. In your Lab Report file, **describe** some of the search results.

▶ **Note:**

This completes the lab. **Close** the **Web browser**, if you have not already done so.

Evaluation Criteria and Rubrics

The following are the evaluation criteria for this lab that students must perform:

1. Review a Zenmap® GUI (Nmap) network discovery and port scanning report and a Nessus® software vulnerability report. – **[25%]**
2. Identify hosts, operating systems, services, applications, and open ports on devices from the Zenmap® GUI (Nmap) scan report. – **[25%]**
3. Identify critical, major, and minor software vulnerabilities from the Nessus® vulnerability assessment scan report. – **[25%]**
4. Visit the Common Vulnerabilities and Exposures (CVE) online listing of software vulnerabilities at *http://cve.mitre.org* and learn how to conduct searches on the site. – **[25%]**

Copyright © 2015 by Jones & Bartlett Learning, LLC, an Ascend Learning Company. All rights reserved.
www.jblearning.com

Lab #5 - Assessment Worksheet

Identifying Risks, Threats, and Vulnerabilities in an IT Infrastructure Using Zenmap® GUI (Nmap) and Nessus® Reports

Course Name and Number: _____

Student Name: _____

Instructor Name: _____

Lab Due Date: _____

Overview

In this lab, you looked at an Nmap® report and a Nessus® report. You visited the *http://cve.mitre.org* Web site, you defined vulnerability and exposure according to the site, and you learned how to conduct searches of the Common Vulnerabilities and Exposures (CVE) listing.

Lab Assessment Questions & Answers

1. Describe the purpose of a Zenmap® GUI (Nmap) report and Nessus® report?

2. Review the Lab 5 Nmap Scan Report. On page 6, what ports and services are enabled on the Cisco Adaptive Security Appliance device?

3. Review the Lab 5 Nmap Scan Report. On page 6, what is the source IP address of the Cisco Adaptive Security Appliance device?

4. How many IP hosts were identified in the Lab 5 Nessus Vulnerability Scan Report? List them.

5. When you identify a known software vulnerability, where can you go to assess the risk impact of the software vulnerability?

6. Define CVE.

7. Explain how the CVE search listing can be a tool for security practitioners and a tool for hackers.

Copyright © 2015 by Jones & Bartlett Learning, LLC, an Ascend Learning Company. All rights reserved.
www.jblearning.com

Lab #6 Developing a Risk-Mitigation Plan Outline for an IT Infrastructure

Introduction

Identifying and assessing risks is challenging, but treating them is another matter entirely. Treating risks means making changes based on a risk assessment and probably a few hard decisions. When treating even the most straightforward of risks, practice due diligence by documenting what steps you are taking to mitigate the risk. If you don't document the change and the reasoning behind it, it's possible that your organization could reverse the mitigation and reintroduce the risk based on the notion of "but that's how we always did it before."

After you've addressed a risk, appoint someone to make certain that the risk treatment is being regularly applied. If a security incident arises even with the change in place, having a single person in charge will ensure that any corrective action aligns with the risk-mitigation plan. You're not appointing someone so you can blame that person if things go wrong; you are instead investing that individual with the autonomy to manage the incident effectively. The purpose of a risk-mitigation plan is to define and document procedures and processes to establish a baseline for ongoing mitigation of risks in the seven domains of an IT infrastructure.

In this lab, you will identify the scope for an IT risk-mitigation plan, you will align the plan's major parts with the seven domains of an IT infrastructure, you will define the risk-mitigation steps, you will define procedures and processes needed to maintain a security baseline for ongoing mitigation, and you will create an outline for an IT risk-mitigation plan.

Learning Objectives

Upon completing this lab, you will be able to:

- Identify the scope for an IT risk-mitigation plan focusing on the seven domains of a typical IT infrastructure.
- Align the major parts of an IT risk-mitigation plan in each of the seven domains of a typical IT infrastructure.
- Define the tactical risk-mitigation steps needed to remediate the identified risks, threats, and vulnerabilities commonly found in the seven domains of a typical IT infrastructure.
- Define procedures and processes needed to maintain a security baseline definition for ongoing risk mitigation in the seven domains of a typical IT infrastructure.
- Create an outline for an IT risk-mitigation plan encompassing the seven domains of a typical IT infrastructure.

Deliverables

Upon completion of this lab, you are required to provide the following deliverables to your instructor:

1. Lab Report file;
2. Lab Assessments file.

Copyright © 2015 by Jones & Bartlett Learning, LLC, an Ascend Learning Company. All rights reserved.

Hands-On Steps

▶ **Note:**
This is a paper-based lab. To successfully complete the deliverables for this lab, you will need access to Microsoft®
Word or another compatible word processor. For some labs, you may also need access to a graphics line drawing
application, such as Visio or PowerPoint. Refer to the Preface of this manual for information on creating the lab
deliverable files.

1. On your local computer, **create** the **lab deliverable files**.

2. **Review** the **Lab Assessment Worksheet**. You will find answers to these questions as you
    proceed through the lab steps.

3. **Review** the seven domains of a typical IT infrastructure (see Figure 1).

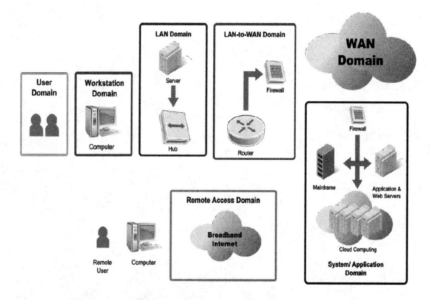

Figure 1 Seven domains of a typical IT infrastructure

4. Using the following table, **review** the results of your assessments in the Performing a
    Qualitative Risk Assessment for an IT Infrastructure lab in this lab manual. In addition,
    review the results of how you categorized and prioritized the risks for the IT infrastructure
    in that lab:

Risks, Threats, and Vulnerabilities	Primary Domain Impacted	Risk Impact/ Factor
Unauthorized access from public Internet		
User destroys data in application and deletes all files		
Hacker penetrates your IT infrastructure and gains access to your internal network		
Intraoffice employee romance gone bad		
Fire destroys primary data center		
Service provider service level agreement (SLA) is not achieved		
Workstation operating system (OS) has a known software vulnerability		
Unauthorized access to organization-owned workstations		
Loss of production data		
Denial of service attack on organization Demilitarized Zone (DMZ) and e-mail server		
Remote communications from home office		
Local Area Network (LAN) server OS has a known software vulnerability		
User downloads and clicks on an unknown e-mail attachment		
Workstation browser has a software vulnerability		
Mobile employee needs secure browser access to sales-order entry system		
Service provider has a major network outage		
Weak ingress/egress traffic-filtering degrades performance		
User inserts CDs and USB hard drives with personal photos, music, and videos on organization-owned computers		
Virtual Private Network (VPN) tunneling between remote computer and ingress/egress router is needed		
Wireless Local Area Network (WLAN) access points are needed for LAN connectivity within a warehouse		
Need to prevent eavesdropping on WLAN due to customer privacy data access		
Denial of service (DoS)/distributed denial of service (DDoS) attack from the Wide Area Network (WAN)/Internet		

Copyright © 2015 by Jones & Bartlett Learning, LLC, an Ascend Learning Company. All rights reserved.
www.jblearning.com

5. In your Lab Report file, **organize** the qualitative risk assessment data according to the following:

   - **Review** the executive summary from the Performing a Qualitative Risk Assessment for an IT Infrastructure lab in this lab manual.
   - **Organize** all of the critical "1" risks, threats, and vulnerabilities identified throughout the seven domains of a typical IT infrastructure.

Fighting Fear

In the real world, some managers will accept risk rather than make changes to mitigate it. If they offer up only vague reasons for sticking with the status quo, then their decision is likely based on fear of change. Don't let their fear stop you from treating the risk.

Here are two tips to fight a manager's fear:

- Prepare for your manager's "What if?" questions. Example of a manager's question: "What if we apply the firewall but it also stops network traffic we want, such as from our applications?" Your answer: "We've tested nearly all applications with the chosen firewall. And we're prepared to minimize unforeseen outages."
- Know, in concrete terms, what will happen if the risk is not treated. Example of a manager's question: "What is supposed to happen that hasn't happened already?" Your answer will come from the risk assessment you've performed, which will calculate the risk's likelihood and consequences.

---

6. On your local computer, **open** a new **Internet browser window**.

7. In the address box of your Internet browser, **type** the URL **http://www.mitre.org/publications/systems-engineering-guide/acquisition-systems-engineering/risk-management/risk-impact-assessment-and-prioritization** and **press Enter** to open the Web site.

8. **Read** the article titled "Risk Impact Assessment and Prioritization."

9. In your Lab Report file, **describe** the purpose of prioritizing the risks prior to creating a risk-mitigation plan.

10. In your Lab Report file, **describe** the elements of an IT risk-mitigation plan outline by covering the following major topics:

    - Executive summary
    - Prioritization of identified risks, threats, and vulnerabilities organized into the seven domains
    - Critical "1" risks, threats, and vulnerabilities identified throughout the IT infrastructure
    - Short-term remediation steps for critical "1" risks, threats, and vulnerabilities
    - Long-term remediation steps for major "2" and minor "3" risks, threats, and vulnerabilities
    - Ongoing IT risk-mitigation steps for the seven domains of a typical IT infrastructure
    - Cost magnitude estimates for work effort and security solutions

- Implementation plans for remediation

11. In your Lab Report file, **create** a detailed IT risk-mitigation plan outline by inserting appropriate subtopics and sub-bullets.

> ▶**Note:**
> This completes the lab. **Close** the **Web browser**, if you have not already done so.

Copyright © 2015 by Jones & Bartlett Learning, LLC, an Ascend Learning Company. All rights reserved.
www.jblearning.com

Evaluation Criteria and Rubrics

The following are the evaluation criteria for this lab that students must perform:

1. Identify the scope for an IT risk-mitigation plan focusing on the seven domains of a typical IT infrastructure. – **[20%]**
2. Align the major parts of an IT risk-mitigation plan in each of the seven domains of a typical IT infrastructure. – **[20%]**
3. Define the tactical risk-mitigation steps needed to remediate the identified risks, threats, and vulnerabilities commonly found in the seven domains of a typical IT infrastructure. – **[20%]**
4. Define procedures and processes needed to maintain a security baseline definition for ongoing risk mitigation in the seven domains of a typical IT infrastructure. – **[20%]**
5. Create an outline for an IT risk-mitigation plan encompassing the seven domains of a typical IT infrastructure. – **[20%]**

Lab #6 - Assessment Worksheet

Developing a Risk-Mitigation Plan Outline for an IT Infrastructure

Course Name and Number: _____

Student Name: _____

Instructor Name: _____

Lab Due Date: _____

Overview

In this lab, you identified the scope for an IT risk-mitigation plan, you aligned the plan's major parts with the seven domains of an IT infrastructure, you defined the risk-mitigation steps, you defined procedures and processes needed to maintain a security baseline for ongoing mitigation, and you created an outline for an IT risk-mitigation plan.

Lab Assessment Questions & Answers

1. Why is it important to prioritize your IT infrastructure risks, threats, and vulnerabilities?

2. Based on your executive summary produced in the Performing a Qualitative Risk Assessment for an IT Infrastructure lab in this lab manual, what is the primary focus of your message to executive management?

3. Given the scenario for your IT risk-mitigation plan, what influence did your scenario have on prioritizing your identified risks, threats, and vulnerabilities?

4. What risk-mitigation solutions do you recommend for handling the following risk element: User inserts CDs and USB hard drives with personal photos, music, and videos on organization-owned computers?

Copyright © 2015 by Jones & Bartlett Learning, LLC, an Ascend Learning Company. All rights reserved.

5. What is a security baseline definition?

6. What questions do you have for executive management to finalize your IT risk-mitigation plan?

7. What is the most important risk-mitigation requirement you uncovered and want to communicate to executive management? In your opinion, why is this the most important risk-mitigation requirement?

8. Based on your IT risk-mitigation plan, what is the difference between short-term and long-term risk-mitigation tasks and ongoing duties?

9. For which of the seven domains of a typical IT infrastructure is it easy to implement risk-mitigation solutions but difficult to monitor and track effectiveness?

10. Which of the seven domains of a typical IT infrastructure usually contains privacy data in systems, servers, and databases?

11. Which of the seven domains of a typical IT infrastructure can access privacy data and also store it on local hard drives and disks?

12. Why is the Remote Access Domain the most risk-prone of all in a typical IT infrastructure?

13. When considering the implementation of software updates, software patches, and software fixes, why must you test the upgrade or software patch before you implement it as a risk-mitigation tactic?

14. Are risk-mitigation policies, standards, procedures, and guidelines needed as part of your long-term risk-mitigation plan? Why or why not?

15. If an organization under a compliance law is not in compliance, how critical is it for your organization to mitigate this noncompliance risk element?

Copyright © 2015 by Jones & Bartlett Learning, LLC, an Ascend Learning Company. All rights reserved.

© Rodolfo Clix/Dreamstime.com

Lab #7 Performing a Business Impact Analysis for a Mock IT Infrastructure

Introduction

The purpose of a business impact analysis (BIA) is to identify applications and data access requirements in an IT infrastructure. The BIA helps you assess affected IT systems, applications, and resources and align them with their required recovery time objectives (RTOs). It then helps you prioritize the identified mission-critical business functions so you know how IT systems, applications, and resources are impacted.

In this lab, you will define a BIA's goal and objective, you will identify where the BIA fits in the business continuity plan (BCP), you will identify mission-critical applications and data access requirements, you will perform a BIA qualitative assessment approach, and you will create a BIA executive summary report for management.

Learning Objectives

Upon completing this lab, you will be able to:

- Define the goal and objective of a business impact analysis (BIA).
- Identify where a business impact analysis (BIA) fits within a business continuity plan (BCP).
- Identify mission-critical applications and access to data requirements for a given scenario.
- Perform a business impact analysis (BIA) utilizing a qualitative assessment approach.
- Create a business impact analysis executive summary report for management.

Deliverables

Upon completion of this lab, you are required to provide the following deliverables to your instructor:

1. Lab Report file;
2. Lab Assessments file.

Copyright © 2015 by Jones & Bartlett Learning, LLC, an Ascend Learning Company. All rights reserved.

Hands-On Steps

> ▶**Note:**
> This is a paper-based lab. To successfully complete the deliverables for this lab, you will need access to Microsoft® Word or another compatible word processor. For some labs, you may also need access to a graphics line drawing application, such as Visio or PowerPoint. Refer to the Preface of this manual for information on creating the lab deliverable files.

1. On your local computer, **create** the **lab deliverable files**.

2. **Review** the **Lab Assessment Worksheet**. You will find answers to these questions as you proceed through the lab steps.

3. On your local computer, **open** a new **Internet browser window**.

4. Using your favorite search engine, **search for information** on a **business impact analysis (BIA)**.

5. In your Lab Report file, **define BIA**.

6. Using your favorite search engine, **search for information** on a **business continuity plan (BCP)**.

7. In your Lab Report file, **define BCP** and **explain** how a BIA fits within a BCP.

8. **Review** the business functions in the following table:

Business Functions
Internal and external voice communication with customers in real time
Internal and external e-mail communication with customers via store and forward messaging
Domain Name Server (DNS) for internal and external Internet Protocol (IP) communications
Internet connectivity for e-mail and store and forward customer service
Self-service Web site for customer access to information and personal account information
e-Commerce site for online customer purchases or scheduling 24 x 7 x 365
Payroll and human resources for employees
Real-time customer service via Web site, e-mail, or telephone requires customer relationship management (CRM)
Network management and technical support
Marketing and events
Sales orders or customer/student registration
Remote branch office sales-order entry to headquarters
Voice and e-mail communications to remote branches
Accounting and finance support: Accounts payable, Accounts receivable, etc.

9. In your Lab Report file, **list** a qualitative business impact value of Critical, Major, Minor, or None for each function.

▶**Note:**
For a descriptive comparison of qualitative versus quantitative risk assessment, read this article:
http://www.sans.edu/research/leadership-laboratory/article/risk-assessment.

10. In your Lab Report file, **list** the IT systems, applications, and resources that are impacted for each of the functions.

11. In the address box of your Internet browser, **type** the URL **http://searchdisasterrecovery.techtarget.com/feature/Using-a-business-impact-analysis-BIA-template-A-free-BIA-template-and-guide/** and **press Enter** to open the Web site.

12. **Read** the article titled "Using a business impact analysis (BIA) template" for guidance on writing a business impact analysis. **Consult** the article for the meaning of the terms recovery time objective (RTO) and recovery point objective (RPO).

13. In your Lab Report file, **assess** the recovery time objectives (RTO) for each of the impacted IT systems, applications, and resources.

14. **Write** a four-paragraph **executive summary** that includes the following:

- Goals and purpose of the BIA (unique to your scenario)
- Summary of findings (business functions and assessment)
- Prioritizations (critical, major, and minor classifications)
- IT systems and applications impacted (to support the defined recovery time objectives)

▶**Note:**
This completes the lab. **Close** the **Web browser**, if you have not already done so.

Copyright © 2015 by Jones & Bartlett Learning, LLC, an Ascend Learning Company. All rights reserved.
www.jblearning.com

Evaluation Criteria and Rubrics

The following are the evaluation criteria for this lab that students must perform:

1. Define the goal and objective of a business impact analysis (BIA). – **[20%]**
2. Identify where a business impact analysis (BIA) fits within a business continuity plan (BCP). – **[20%]**
3. Identify mission-critical applications and access to data requirements for a given scenario. – **[20%]**
4. Perform a business impact analysis (BIA) utilizing a qualitative assessment approach. – **[20%]**
5. Create a business impact analysis executive summary report for management. – **[20%]**

Lab #7 - Assessment Worksheet

Performing a Business Impact Analysis for a Mock IT Infrastructure

Course Name and Number: _____

Student Name: _____

Instructor Name: _____

Lab Due Date: _____

Overview

In this lab, you defined a BIA's goal and objective, you identified where the BIA fits in the business continuity plan (BCP), you identified mission-critical applications and data access requirements, you performed a BIA qualitative assessment approach, and you created a BIA executive summary report for management.

Lab Assessment Questions & Answers

1. What is the goal and purpose of a business impact analysis (BIA)?

2. Why is a business impact analysis (BIA) an important first step in defining a business continuity plan (BCP)?

3. What is the definition of recovery time objective (RTO)? Why is this important to define in an IT Security Policy Definition as part of the business impact analysis (BIA) or business continuity plan (BCP)?

4. How do risk management and risk assessment relate to a business impact analysis (BIA) for an IT infrastructure?

Copyright © 2015 by Jones & Bartlett Learning, LLC, an Ascend Learning Company. All rights reserved.
www.jblearning.com

5. True or false: If the recovery point objective (RPO) metric does not equal the recovery time objective (RTO), you can potentially lose data that might not be backed up. This represents a gap in potential lost or unrecoverable data.

6. If you have an RPO of 0 hours, what does that mean?

7. What must you explain to executive management when defining RTO and RPO objectives for the BIA?

8. What questions do you have for executive management in order to finalize your BIA?

9. Why do customer service business functions typically have a short RTO and RPO maximum allowable time objective?

10. To write backup and recovery procedures, you need to review the IT systems, hardware, software, and communications infrastructure that supports business operations and functions, and you need to define how to maximize availability. This alignment of IT systems and components must be based on business operations, functions, and prioritizations. This prioritization is usually the result of a risk assessment and how those risks, threats, and vulnerabilities impact business operations and functions. What is the proper sequence of development and implementation for the following plans?:

    - Business Continuity Plan:
    - Disaster Recovery Plan:
    - Risk Management Plan:
    - Business Impact Analysis:

© Rodolfo Clix/Dreamstime.com

Lab #8 Developing an Outline for a Business Continuity Plan for an IT Infrastructure

Introduction

All businesses are at peak performance when things run smoothly, but it's a well-planned business that can still perform after a serious disruption. Every business experiences outages or disruptions at some level. Minor disruptions are so commonplace, in fact, that they're "just a part of doing business."

Examples of minor disruptions range from employee turnover to a supplier changing its prices to a busted microwave in the office kitchen. More significant disruptions include losing valuable executives, experiencing serious market volatility, or facing a massive water leak in the office or warehouse. Finally, the worst-case disasters that can completely halt business include a major fire or a flu pandemic.

Business continuity describes the set of processes an organization must act on when disruptions occur. For the worst-case scenarios, business continuity is labeled disaster recovery, but business continuity generally means continuing business for any disruption significant enough to benefit from planning. No type of planning is more important to an organization than business continuity and disaster recovery planning. The purpose of a business continuity plan (BCP) is to identify and assess the risks, threats, and vulnerabilities that threaten a company so you can minimize both internal and external exposure to them and so you can mitigate them. A BCP's goal is to document processes for prevention and recovery.

In this lab, you will explain a BCP's goals, you will align a business impact analysis (BIA) with the BCP's scope, you will identify the BCP's major parts, and you will develop a BCP outline for a given scenario.

Learning Objectives

Upon completing this lab, you will be able to:

- Define the goals and purpose of a business continuity plan (BCP) for an IT infrastructure.
- Align a business impact analysis (BIA) to define the scope of a business continuity plan (BCP) for an IT infrastructure.
- Identify the major parts of a business continuity plan (BCP) unique to the scenario and IT infrastructure.
- Develop a business continuity plan (BCP) outline for a given scenario and vertical industry.

Deliverables

Upon completion of this lab, you are required to provide the following deliverables to your instructor:

1. Lab Report file;
2. Lab Assessments file.

Hands-On Steps

> **▶ Note:**
> This is a paper-based lab. To successfully complete the deliverables for this lab, you will need access to Microsoft® Word or another compatible word processor. For some labs, you may also need access to a graphics line drawing application, such as Visio or PowerPoint. Refer to the Preface of this manual for information on creating the lab deliverable files.

1. On your local computer, **create** the **lab deliverable files**.

2. **Review** the **Lab Assessment Worksheet**. You will find answers to these questions as you proceed through the lab steps.

3. **Review** the Mock IT infrastructure for a health care IT infrastructure servicing patients with life-threatening conditions (see Figure 1).

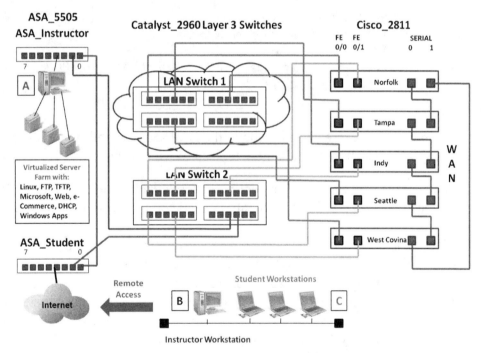

Figure 1 Mock IT infrastructure

4. In your Lab Report file, **describe** some of the major threats and vulnerabilities that might threaten areas of the Mock IT infrastructure in Figure 1.

Copyright © 2015 by Jones & Bartlett Learning, LLC, an Ascend Learning Company. All rights reserved.

> ▶**Note:**
> To identify critical business function areas subject to threats, consider what systems or processes are essential to business operations and are also single points of failure.

5. On your local computer, **open** a new **Internet browser window**.

6. Using your favorite search engine, **search for information** on a **business impact analysis (BIA)**.

7. In your Lab Report file, **define BIA**.

8. Using your favorite search engine, **search for information** on a **business continuity plan (BCP)**.

9. In your Lab Report file, **define BCP** and **explain** how a BIA fits within a BCP.

> ▶**Note:**
> In real-world scenarios, BCP testing should be as authentic as possible. Caution: It's a thin line between genuinely testing your BCP and inadvertently causing an unrecoverable business disruption.
>
> After every BCP test, however small, you will learn some lessons. Add these details to your BCP document after having tested it. Every detail can help minimize recovery time.

10. In your Lab Report file, **create** an **outline** of the BCP sections and subtopics that apply to the Mock IT infrastructure. **Include** these topics in your outline:

   - **Initiation of the BCP** (introduction, definitions, relevant policy statements, BCP organizational structure, BCP declaration, BCP communications, and information sharing)
   - **Business Impact Analysis** (risk assessment and analysis prioritizing business functions and operations aligned to IT systems, applications, and resources)
   - **Business Continuity/Disaster Readiness/Recovery** (recovery time objective [RTO], recovery point objective [RPO], business continuity benchmarks, disaster recovery planning [DRP as a subset of a BCP plan], and recovery steps and procedures for mission-critical IT systems, applications, and data)
   - **Develop and Implement the Plan** (the plan is a living and breathing document that requires annual updates and change control revisions; implementation and the instructions for how to engage the BCP are part of this section)
   - **Test and Update the Plan** (the most important part of a BCP or DRP is to test the plan with a "mock" business continuity disruption or disaster scenario; tabletop reviews of the processes and procedures can be conducted to inform all BCP and DRP team members of their roles, responsibilities, and accountabilities)

Note:
This completes the lab. **Close** the **Web browser**, if you have not already dono co.

Copyright © 2015 by Jones & Bartlett Learning, LLC, an Ascend Learning Company. All rights reserved.

Evaluation Criteria and Rubrics

The following are the evaluation criteria for this lab that students must perform:

1. Define the goals and purpose of a business continuity plan (BCP) for an IT infrastructure. – **[25%]**
2. Align a business impact analysis (BIA) to define the scope of a business continuity plan (BCP) for an IT infrastructure. – **[25%]**
3. Identify the major parts of a business continuity plan (BCP) unique to the scenario and IT infrastructure. – **[25%]**
4. Develop a business continuity plan (BCP) outline for a given scenario and vertical industry. – **[25%]**

Lab #8 - Assessment Worksheet

Developing an Outline for a Business Continuity Plan for an IT Infrastructure

Course Name and Number: _____

Student Name: _____

Instructor Name: _____

Lab Due Date: _____

Overview

In this lab, you explained a BCP's goals, you aligned a business impact analysis (BIA) with the BCP's scope, you identified the BCP's major parts, and you developed a BCP outline for a given scenario.

Lab Assessment Questions & Answers

1. How does a BCP help mitigate risk?

2. What kind of risk does a BCP help mitigate?

3. If you have business liability insurance, asset replacement insurance, and natural disaster insurance, do you still need a BCP or disaster recovery plan (DRP)? Why or why not?

4. From your scenario and BIA from the Performing a Business Impact Analysis for a Mock IT Infrastructure lab in this lab manual, what were the mission-critical business functions and operations you identified? Are these the focus of your BCP?

5. What does a BIA help define for a BCP?

Copyright © 2015 by Jones & Bartlett Learning, LLC, an Ascend Learning Company. All rights reserved.
www.jblearning.com

6. Who should develop and participate in an organization's BCP?

7. Why do disaster planning and disaster recovery belong in a BCP?

8. What is the purpose of having documented IT system, application, and data recovery procedures and steps?

9. Why must you include testing of the plan in your BCP?

10. How often should you update your BCP document?

11. In your BCP outline, where will you find a list of prioritized business operations, functions, and processes?

12. In your BCP outline, where will you find detailed backup and system recovery information?

13. In your BCP outline, where will you find a policy definition defining how to engage your BCP due to a major outage or disaster?

14. In your BCP outline, where will you find a policy definition defining the resources that are needed to perform the tasks associated with business continuity or disaster recovery?

15. What is the purpose of testing your BCP and DRP procedures, backups, and recovery steps?

© Rodolfo Clix/Dreamstime.com

Lab #9 Developing Disaster Recovery Backup Procedures and Recovery Instructions

Introduction

When disaster strikes a business, executive management expects its IT team has a recovery plan prepped and ready to go. A successful recovery hinges in part on whether IT has properly tested its plan and regularly updated it. Recovery speed is also key.

The purpose of a business continuity and disaster recovery plan is to document all identified mission-critical IT systems, applications, and data recovery procedures. Fast recovery times for IT systems and applications are achievable with efficient and accurate recovery instructions.

In this lab, you will apply the same concepts of disaster recovery backup procedures and recovery instructions to your own data. You will explain how you can lower recovery time objectives (RTOs) with proper backup and recovery procedures, you will define a process for IT system and application recovery procedures, you will identify a backup solution for saving your own data, and you will test and verify your backups for RTO compliance.

Learning Objectives

Upon completing this lab, you will be able to:

- Explain how to lower RTO with properly documented backup and recovery steps.
- Define a process for IT system and application recovery procedures.
- Identify a backup solution for saving Lab Assessment Worksheets on a system other than your Student VM workstation and hard drive.
- Test and validate your basic backup and recovery procedures for saving Lab Assessment Worksheets on an alternate system or solution other than your existing hard drive.
- Test the backup and recovery procedures for RTO compliance.

Deliverables

Upon completion of this lab, you are required to provide the following deliverables to your instructor:

1. Lab Report file;
2. Lab Assessments file.

Hands-On Steps

▶ **Note:**

This is a paper-based lab. To successfully complete the deliverables for this lab, you will need access to Microsoft® Word or another compatible word processor. For some labs, you may also need access to a graphics line drawing application, such as Visio or PowerPoint. Refer to the Preface of this manual for information on creating the lab deliverable files.

1. On your local computer, **create** the **lab deliverable files**.

2. **Review** the **Lab Assessment Worksheet**. You will find answers to these questions as you proceed through the lab steps.

3. On your local computer, **open** a new **Internet browser window**.

4. Using your favorite search engine, **search for information** on **recovery time objective (RTO)**.

5. **Briefly review** at least three of the first page results regarding RTO.

6. In the address box of your Internet browser, **type** the URL **http://www.bluelock.com/blog/rpo-rto-pto-and-raas-disaster-recovery-explained/ and press Enter to open the Web site**.

7. **Read** the article titled "**RPO, RTO, PTO and RaaS: Disaster recovery explained.**"

8. In the address box of your Internet browser, **type** the URL **http://www.computerweekly.com/feature/How-to-write-a-disaster-recovery-plan-and-define-disaster-recovery-strategies/ and press Enter to open the Web site**.

9. **Read** the article regarding disaster recovery strategies.

10. **Make** a backup of any Lab Assessment Worksheets you may have completed from this lab manual. If this is the only lab you've worked on, then make a mock Lab Assessment Worksheet using the worksheet from this lab and back that one up instead.

11. **Attach** the file(s) to an e-mail to your personal e-mail address. You may need to send multiple e-mails depending on your e-mail's size limitations.

▶ **Note:**

At this point, ask yourself questions from the perspective of recovering from a disaster: Would I be able to access this e-mail from an offsite computer? Where is the e-mail stored? If I were incapacitated, is someone else able to proceed without me? This is the mindset of someone crafting business continuity plans.

12. **Verify** receipt of the e-mail message(s), and then **open** and **verify** file integrity for each attachment.

13. In your Lab Report file, **write** the backup procedures and recovery procedures you used.

> ▶**Note:**
> Arguably, the most important section of any business continuity plan is the Procedures section. A business can plan disaster recovery scenarios extensively, carefully weighing all possible risk likelihood and impacts. However, without detailed procedures with which to execute the recovery, a business will not resume operations efficiently, if at all. And this is especially true in times of near-panic and extreme "executive oversight" immediately following a disaster. The key source for documenting accurate and helpful recovery procedures is testing.

14. In your Lab Report file, **describe** your personal procedures in terms of your RTO as explained in Web sites visited earlier in this lab.

15. **Test** your backup and recovery procedures per your RTO.

16. In your Lab Report file, **describe** ways you can lower the RTO.

> ▶**Note:**
> This completes the lab. **Close** the **Web browser**, if you have not already done so.

Evaluation Criteria and Rubrics

The following are the evaluation criteria for this lab that students must perform:

1. Explain how to lower RTO with properly documented backup and recovery steps. – **[20%]**
2. Define a process for IT system and application recovery procedures. – **[20%]**
3. Identify a backup solution for saving all of your Lab Assessment Worksheets on a system other than your Student VM workstation and hard drive. – **[20%]**
4. Test and validate your basic backup and recovery procedures for saving your Lab Assessment Worksheets on an alternate system or solution other than your existing hard drive. – **[20%]**
5. Test the backup and recovery procedures for RTO compliance. – **[20%]**

Copyright © 2015 by Jones & Bartlett Learning, LLC, an Ascend Learning Company. All rights reserved.
www.jblearning.com

Lab #9 - Assessment Worksheet

Developing Disaster Recovery Backup Procedures and Recovery Instructions

Course Name and Number: _____

Student Name: _____

Instructor Name: _____

Lab Due Date: _____

Overview

In this lab, you applied the same concepts of disaster recovery backup procedures and recovery instructions to your own data. You explained how you can lower recovery time objectives (RTOs) with proper backup and recovery procedures, you defined a process for IT system and application recovery procedures, you identified a backup solution for saving your own data, and you tested and verified your backups for RTO compliance.

Lab Assessment Questions & Answers

1. How do documented backup and recovery procedures help achieve RTO?

2. True or false: To achieve an RTO of 0, you need 100 percent redundant, hot-stand-by infrastructure (that is, IT systems, applications, data, and so on).

3. What is most important when considering data backups?

4. What is most important when considering data recovery?

5. What are the risks of using your external e-mail box as a backup and data storage solution?

6. Identify the total amount of time required to recover and install the Lab Assessment Worksheet(s) and to open the file(s) to verify integrity. (Calculate your timed RTO using your computer clock and your documented instructions.)

7. Did you achieve your RTO? What steps and procedures can you implement to help drive RTO even lower?

8. What are some recommendations for lowering the RTO for retrieval and access to the backup data file?

9. If you drive RTO lower, what must you do to streamline the procedure?

10. Why are documenting and testing critical to achieve a defined RTO?

11. Why is it a best practice for an organization to document its backup and recovery steps for disaster recovery?

12. What can you do to cut down on the recovery time for accessing, copying, and recovering your Lab Assessment Worksheets to achieve the RTO?

13. What will encryption of a disk or data in storage do to the RTO definition when attempting to retrieve and recover cleartext data for production use?

14. How many total steps did your backup and recovery procedures consist of for this lab exercise? Are there any that can be combined or streamlined?

Copyright © 2015 by Jones & Bartlett Learning, LLC, an Ascend Learning Company. All rights reserved.
www.jblearning.com

15. If the individual accessing the system for disaster recovery purposes were not familiar with the IT system and required system administrator logon credentials, what additional step would be required in the recovery phase?

Lab #10 Creating a CIRT Response Plan for a Typical IT Infrastructure

Introduction

When a company experiences a computer incident, its security team that collects and monitors incidents must make a decision. That decision is whether the incident is benign, or whether it signals a greater problem, such as an attempted (or successful) security breach.

When people hear "security breach," they often imagine sinister hackers bypassing firewalls to steal top secret plans. The attack might be one of thousands, a "noisy" spray of exploits across a network. Or the attack might be targeted solely at one company and, as the attacker hopes, more stealthy.

In any case, as different pieces of evidence are collected, it becomes easier to confirm whether a breach really has occurred and, if so, how it must be handled by a specialized team of security professionals. These special teams are referred to as computer incident response teams (CIRTs). A CIRT team operates on the actions laid out in a CIRT plan. The purpose of a computer incident response team (CIRT) plan is to mitigate risks found in the seven domains of a typical IT infrastructure.

When tasked to manage a security breach, a CIRT team will identify, analyze, and contain the extent of the security breach. Then they will get rid of the breach and whatever traces—a virus or other malware—were left behind. Next, as some business functions might have been affected, the CIRT team helps recover from the breach. Lastly, the CIRT team discusses and improves its CIRT plan based on lessons learned during a review session.

In this lab, you will explain how CIRT plans mitigate risks, you will identify where CIRT monitoring and security operation tasks occur throughout an IT infrastructure, you will identify the security controls and countermeasures that mitigate risk, and you will create a CIRT response plan.

Learning Objectives

Upon completing this lab, you will be able to:

- Explain how a CIRT plan can help mitigate risks found in the seven domains of a typical IT infrastructure.

- Identify where CIRT monitoring and security operation tasks occur throughout an IT infrastructure.
- Identify security controls and security countermeasures to mitigate risk throughout the IT infrastructure and to aid in security incident response.
- Create a CIRT response plan for the Mock IT infrastructure by using the six-step incident-response methodology.

Deliverables

Upon completion of this lab, you are required to provide the following deliverables to your instructor:

1. Lab Report file;
2. Lab Assessments file.

Copyright © 2015 by Jones & Bartlett Learning, LLC, an Ascend Learning Company. All rights reserved.

Hands-On Steps

> ▶**Note:**
> This is a paper-based lab. To successfully complete the deliverables for this lab, you will need access to Microsoft® Word or another compatible word processor. For some labs, you may also need access to a graphics line drawing application, such as Visio or PowerPoint. Refer to the Preface of this manual for information on creating the lab deliverable files.

1. On your local computer, **create** the **lab deliverable files**.

2. **Review** the **Lab Assessment Worksheet**. You will find answers to these questions as you proceed through the lab steps.

3. **Review** the Mock IT infrastructure for a health care IT infrastructure servicing patients with life-threatening conditions (see Figure 1).

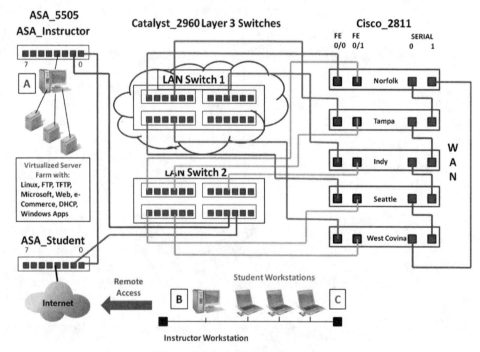

Figure 1 Mock IT infrastructure

4. In your Lab Report file, **identify** and then **document** the security controls and security countermeasures you can implement throughout Figure 1 to help mitigate risk from unauthorized access and access to intellectual property or customer privacy data.

5. **Review** the steps for creating a CIRT plan as outlined in the following table:

Step	Description of Step
Preparation	What tools, applications, laptops, and communication devices are needed to address computer/security incident response for this specific breach?
Identification	When an incident is reported, it must be identified, classified, and documented. During this step, the following information is needed: validating the incident; identifying its nature, if an incident has occurred; identifying and protecting the evidence; and logging and reporting the event or incident.
Containment	The immediate objective is to limit the scope and magnitude of the computer/security-related incident as quickly as possible, rather than allow the incident to continue to gain evidence for identifying and/or prosecuting the perpetrator.
Eradication	The next priority is to remove the computer/security-related incident or breach's effects.
Recovery	Recovery is specific to bringing back into production those IT systems, applications, and assets that were affected by the security-related incident.
Post-Mortem Review	Following up on an incident after the recovery tasks and services are completed is a critical last step in the overall methodology. A post-mortem report should include a complete explanation of the incident and the resolution and applicable configuration management, security countermeasures, and implementation recommendations to prevent the security incident or breach from occurring again.

▶**Note:**

The post-mortem review is arguably the most important step as CIRT team members re-evaluate their actions with the valuable luxury of hindsight. When the CIRT members are able to look back to compare what they saw and how it related to what happened next, they can continually improve what they offer the organization.

Copyright © 2015 by Jones & Bartlett Learning, LLC, an Ascend Learning Company. All rights reserved.

6. In your Lab Report file, **create** a CIRT response plan approach according to the six-step methodology unique to the risks associated with the item you choose from the following:

- Internet ingress/egress at ASA_Student
- Headquarters' departmental VLANs on LAN Switch 1 and 2 with cleartext privacy data
- Remote branch office locations connected through the WAN
- Data center/server farm at ASA_Instructor

> ▶**Note:**
> This completes the lab. **Close** the **Web browser**, if you have not already done so.

Evaluation Criteria and Rubrics

The following are the evaluation criteria for this lab that students must perform:

1. Explain how a CIRT plan can help mitigate risks found in the seven domains of a typical IT infrastructure. – **[25%]**
2. Identify where CIRT monitoring and security operation tasks occur throughout an IT infrastructure. – **[25%]**
3. Identify security controls and security countermeasures to mitigate risk throughout the IT infrastructure and to aid in security incident response. – **[25%]**
4. Create a CIRT response plan for the Mock IT infrastructure by using the six-step incident-response methodology. – **[25%]**

Copyright © 2015 by Jones & Bartlett Learning, LLC, an Ascend Learning Company. All rights reserved.

Lab #10 - Assessment Worksheet

Creating a CIRT Response Plan for a Typical IT Infrastructure

Course Name and Number: _____

Student Name: _____

Instructor Name: _____

Lab Due Date: _____

Overview

In this lab, you explained how CIRT plans mitigate risks, you identified where CIRT monitoring and security operation tasks occur throughout an IT infrastructure, you identified the security controls and countermeasures that mitigate risk, and you created a CIRT response plan.

Lab Assessment Questions & Answers

1. What risk-mitigation security controls or security countermeasures do you recommend for the portion of the network for which you created a CIRT response plan? Explain your answer.

2. How does a CIRT plan help an organization mitigate risk?

3. How does the CIRT post-mortem review help mitigate risk?

4. Why is it a good idea to have a protocol analyzer as one of your incident response tools when examining Internet Protocol (IP) Local Area Network (LAN) network performance or connectivity issues?

5. Put the following in the proper sequence:

- Identification:
- Containment:
- Post-Mortem Review:
- Eradication:
- Preparation:
- Recovery:

6. Which step in the CIRT response methodology relates back to the recovery time objective (RTO) for critical IT systems?

7. Which step in the CIRT response methodology requires proper handling of digital evidence?

8. Which step in the CIRT response methodology requires review with executive management?

9. Which step in the CIRT response methodology requires security applications and tools readiness?

Copyright © 2015 by Jones & Bartlett Learning, LLC, an Ascend Learning Company. All rights reserved.
www.jblearning.com